INCREDIBLE NATURE

by Kristin Marciniak

12 STORY LIBRARY

www.12StoryLibrary.com

12-Story Library is an imprint of Bookstaves and Press Room Editions

Produced for 12-Story Library by Red Line Editorial

Photographs ©: Incredible Arctic/Shutterstock Images, cover, 1; Krissanapong Wongsawarng/Shutterstock Images, 4; Ross Burgener/ET/NOAA/OAR/ESRL/GMD, 5; Bucchi Francesco/Shutterstock Images, 6, 29; saraporn/Shutterstock Images, 7; Naruden Boonareesirichai/Shutterstock Images, 8; Dan Thornberg/Shutterstock Images, 9; Javier Trueba/MSF/Science Source, 10, 28; tom hollett/Shutterstock Images, 11; Bala Sivakumar CC2.0, 12; Brad Greenlee CC2.0, 13; NASA/GSFC/Maggie McAdam, 14; daveynin CC2.0, 15; ArtTomCat/Shutterstock Images, 16; Susan McKenzie/Shutterstock Images, 17; AlessandroZocc/Shutterstock Images, 18; Ch'ien Lee/Minden Pictures/Newscom, 19; Dick Culbert CC2.0, 20; Mike M CC2.0, 21; Ilya Images/Shutterstock Images, 22; Steve Heap/Shutterstock Images, 23; Saturated/iStockphoto, 24; Elena Giglia CC2.0, 25; Tony Webster CC2.0, 26; Sean MacEntee CC2.0, 27

Content Consultant: Dr. D'Arcy Meyer-Dombard, Associate Professor of Environmental Studies, Department of Earth and Environmental Sciences, University of Illinois at Chicago

Library of Congress Cataloging-in-Publication Data
A catalog record for this book is available from the Library of Congress
978-1-63235-421-1 (hardcover)
978-1-63235-491-4 (paperback)
978-1-62143-543-3 (ebook)

Printed in the United States of America
022017

Access free, up-to-date content on this topic plus a full digital version of this book. Scan the QR code on page 31 or use your school's login at 12StoryLibrary.com.

Table of Contents

Auroras Light Up the Night Sky

Beautiful blues, greens, and reds dance across the dark night sky. These lights are known as auroras. The aurora borealis occurs near the magnetic North Pole. It appears over Alaska, Canada, Scandinavia, and Russia. The aurora australis occurs near the magnetic South Pole.

It appears over Antarctica, Australia, and New Zealand.

Auroras happen when particles from the sun hit Earth's magnetic field. The sun throws out energized particles called solar wind. The solar winds travel out into space. Some are flung toward Earth. They eventually hit Earth's magnetic field.

A lagoon in Iceland reflects the vibrant colors of an aurora borealis.

The aurora australis appeared over the geographic South Pole in 2013.

The magnetic field surrounds the planet. It protects Earth from harmful radiation. The solar wind causes electrons in Earth's magnetic field to move. The electrons collide with nitrogen and oxygen in Earth's atmosphere. During these collisions, the electrons transfer energy to nitrogen and oxygen. Nitrogen and oxygen release that energy as light.

Sometimes there are large storms on the sun. These big sun storms throw out a lot of solar wind. Much of the wind hits Earth's magnetic field. The particles in the magnetic field create light. The light is so strong that people can see it. The color and brightness of the light depend on altitude and on the type of molecules creating it. They also depend on how fast the molecules are moving. Fast-moving molecules create green light. Slow-moving molecules produce red. Nitrogen particles make blue light. The light waves combine in the atmosphere to create auroras.

40,000
Distance, in miles (64,374 km), above Earth the planet's magnetic field extends.

- Auroras are caused by solar wind colliding with Earth's magnetic field.
- Particles in the magnetic field transfer energy to other molecules, which release the energy as light.
- The aurora borealis occurs near the North Pole, and the aurora australis occurs at the South Pole.

5

Bacteria Color the Grand Prismatic Spring

Yellowstone National Park is in Wyoming, Montana, and Idaho. The park is home to thousands of geysers and hot springs. None is quite as beautiful as the rainbow-ringed Grand Prismatic Spring.

What causes this hot spring's natural beauty? Bacteria.

The Grand Prismatic Spring is the largest hot spring in the United States. A magma chamber lies a few

Thousands of visitors come to Yellowstone National Park every year to see the Grand Prismatic Spring.

3

Number of colors bacteria create in the rings of the Grand Prismatic Spring.

- The Grand Prismatic Spring is a hot spring heated by an underground magma chamber.
- At the center, the water is so hot there is little life, but as the water moves outward and cools, more bacteria can survive.
- The bacteria create yellow, orange, and reddish-brown films, making the water appear colored.

The Grand Prismatic Spring is the third-largest hot spring in the world.

miles below its surface. The magma heats the spring's water. The hot water rises from cracks in the ground. At the center of the spring, the water is 189 degrees Fahrenheit (87°C). The water is too hot for much life to survive at that temperature. The water is very clean and clear.

As the water moves outward, it cools. Bacteria that create colored pigments can survive at these slightly cooler temperatures. The first ring is 165 degrees Fahrenheit (74°C). The bacteria that live there form a thin yellow film. The film makes the water appear yellow. Two types of bacteria dominate life in the second ring. They form an orange film. Even more bacteria live in the final ring. It is 131 degrees Fahrenheit (55°C). These bacteria create a reddish-brown film. Colors mix between the rings, creating a rainbow effect.

THINK ABOUT IT

Bacteria in the Grand Prismatic Spring create colored films. The films make the water appear colored. What other living things can significantly change their environments? Research online to find specific examples.

Corn Sweat Heats Up the Midwest

States in the Midwest experience hot, humid summers. Humidity is the amount of water vapor in the air. Water vapor usually comes from evaporation of large bodies of water. But in the Midwest, there is another source: corn.

All plants draw water out of the soil. They use water to survive and grow. Eventually, water reaches the plant's cells above the ground. The plant releases waste water through its leaves. Corn draws a lot of water out of the soil. Because of

The corn plant's broad leaves release a lot of water, increasing humidity.

THINK ABOUT IT

Do crops in your state increase humidity? Research your state's important crops to discover how much humidity they can create.

Corn sweat from large corn fields can make it feel 110 degrees Fahrenheit (43°C) or hotter.

this, it has a lot of water to release through its leaves. Some farmers and scientists call this "corn sweat."

One acre (0.40 ha) of corn releases approximately 3,500 gallons (13,249 L) of water a day. Midwestern farmers planted more than 94 million acres (38 million ha) of corn in 2016. This corn added 329 billion gallons (1.25 trillion L) of water to the air every day.

This water vapor increases humidity. High humidity makes the Midwest feel hotter than it actually is. A temperature of 88 degrees Fahrenheit (31°C) with 40 percent humidity still feels like 88 degrees (31°C). But the same temperature at 75 percent humidity feels like 103 degrees (39°C).

70
Maximum percentage of humidity meteorologists consider comfortable.

- In the Midwest, a lot of humidity comes from corn releasing water into the air.
- Cornfields in the Midwest can create thousands of gallons of corn sweat.
- Additional moisture makes the air feel hotter than the temperature on the thermometer.

Hidden Cave Is Home to Giant Crystals

In 2000, miners in Chihuahua, Mexico, searched deep underground. They were looking for silver and lead. Instead, they found something incredible hundreds of feet below ground.

The miners found a cave filled with the largest crystals in the world.

Some of the crystals are 40 feet (12 m) long. They weigh 55 tons (50 metric t). The crystals range from almost clear to brilliant white. The giants crisscross the cave like gigantic swords.

The crystals look like ice. But the cave feels like fire. It is

The cave's enormous crystals are made of selenite.

20

Times bigger the Chihuahua crystals are than any other crystal discovered before.

- A cave in Chihuahua, Mexico, is home to the largest crystals in the world.
- The cave sits above a magma chamber, which heated the water that filled the cave.
- The crystals grew undisturbed for more than half a million years.

1,000 feet (305 m) below ground. It sits just one mile (1.6 km) above a magma chamber. Inside, the cave is 127 degrees Fahrenheit (53°C). The humidity is close to 100 percent. To spend more than a few minutes in the cave, miners and scientists wear special suits. The suits are filled with water and ice. Even with these suits, the caves are dangerous for humans. They are hot and filled with toxic air. Miners and scientists can stay in them for only 40 minutes before they start to feel sick.

The heat is hazardous to humans. But it is the reason the giant crystals exist at all. The cave used to be filled with water. The magma chamber heated the water. The water contained a chemical called sulfide. The hot water mixed with cooler water full of oxygen. Oxygen and sulfide make selenite. This is a type of mineral. Tiny crystals of the mineral built on one another for 600,000 years. Eventually, the giant crystals formed.

After discovering the cave, the mining company drained it. This was so miners could work. The water will return once their work is done. After that, the crystals will keep growing.

Many crystals can be held in the palm of one's hand.

Lenticular Clouds Are a Science Riddle Come True

What is constantly in motion but stays right where it is? A lenticular cloud. Lenticular clouds appear for only a few hours. And they seem to stay right where they form.

These flat, round clouds usually form near mountains. Strong, warm, wet winds flow over mountaintops. The winds create waves in the atmosphere. These waves are like the waves made by throwing a rock into a pond.

Moist air at the top of the waves changes from a gas

Lenticular clouds sit atop Mount Rainier in Washington.

UNIDENTIFIED FLYING CLOUD?

Many residents of Cape Town, South Africa, panicked in November 2015. Mysterious objects had appeared over their city. Some people thought the huge gray and white disks in the sky were alien ships. This is not unusual. Throughout history, people have mistaken lenticular clouds for alien spacecraft. Cape Town residents were relieved to learn the disks were lenticular clouds.

Sometimes, people mistake unusual-looking lenticular clouds for UFOs.

to a liquid as it cools. This forms a lenticular cloud. Sometimes just one lens-shaped cloud hovers near a mountaintop. Other times, clouds stack atop one another like pancakes. The clouds disappear when the condensed cold air falls to the bottom of the wave.

The airwaves move as long as the wind blows. New air always flows over the top of the waves. The movement creates new clouds as the old ones disappear. This can make a lenticular cloud appear motionless. When the winds stop, the cloud disappears for good.

100
Distance, in miles (161 km), waves in the atmosphere can stretch downwind from a mountain.

- Lenticular clouds form when strong, warm, wet winds flow over a large, vertical object.
- The moist air cools, condenses, and turns into clouds at the top of the wave.
- The cloud disappears when it reaches the bottom of the wave.

Mystery of Moving Stones Is Solved

Something is moving the rocks in Racetrack Playa. This long, flat stretch of land is in Death Valley. The playa is dotted with boulders that have fallen from nearby mountains. These rocks weigh as much as 600 pounds (272 kg). And they somehow seem to move.

The Racetrack Playa stones move themselves every few years. They leave long trails of mud behind them. But no one has witnessed the rocks moving. Scientists have puzzled over the cause of this unseen movement. Could strong winds push the rocks?

13

Average speed, in feet per minute (3.9 m/min.), stones on Racetrack Playa move.

- Racetrack Playa of Death Valley is home to hundreds of moving stones.
- The stones' movement is caused by a rare combination of floating ice and wind.
- When temperatures rise, the only evidence of the stones' movement are ruts in the mud.

Rocks on the Racetrack Playa appear to creep across the flat, dry lakebed.

Many rocks have traveled hundreds of feet across the playa.

DEATH VALLEY

Death Valley straddles the border between California and Nevada. It is the hottest and driest place in North America. Temperatures can reach up to 134 degrees Fahrenheit (57°C). The desert gets less than 2 inches (5 cm) of rain per year.

Floods, perhaps? In 2014, time-lapse photography provided the answer: ice.

Death Valley is a desert. Rain is rare there. When it does rain, water from the mountains flows into Racetrack Playa. It forms a shallow lake. In colder weather, the lake freezes into ice. As the ice melts, it separates into very thin sheets. These sheets can be hundreds of feet across. They float on top of the water's surface.

Mild winds are enough to push the ice against the rocks on the playa.

This pressure sets the rocks into motion. They move slowly, just a number of feet per minute. Then the temperature rises and the water evaporates. All that remains are the telltale ruts in the mud showing where the stones moved.

15

Phytoplankton Light Up Tropical Beaches

The Maldives Islands in the Indian Ocean are full of natural beauty. This is especially true at night. The glassy, turquoise water looks as if it is glowing. And that is because it is.

A blue-green light dots the water and the sand. Tiny living things called phytoplankton create the light. Phytoplankton glow through a chemical process called bioluminescence. They contain two special chemicals: luciferin and luciferase. When combined, these chemicals produce light. Bioluminescent phytoplankton can be found in Australia, Jamaica, Thailand, Vietnam, and even San Diego, California.

Phytoplankton glow softly all night long. They grow brighter when stressed.

Bioluminescent phytoplankton light up the sea in the Maldives.

THINK ABOUT IT

Phytoplankton are only one group of living things that can glow. Can you come up with a few other plants and animals that can also glow? Research online to create your list.

Bioluminescent phytoplankton add color to the crests of waves in the Pacific Ocean.

Gentle waves or a hungry fish can cause stress. So can curious humans. When stepped on, phytoplankton on the shore twinkle like stars.

Scientists think plankton use the light to scare away predators. They might also use it to attract their predators' predators. For example, the plankton might glow more brightly when a hungry fish approaches. The light might attract a larger fish to eat the first fish.

50
Percentage of the oxygen in Earth's atmosphere phytoplankton create.

- Phytoplankton give off light through a process called bioluminescence.
- They glow brighter when stressed.
- Phytoplankton can be found around the world.

17

Pitcher Plants Dare to Dine Differently

Most plants rely on sunlight and water for energy. But not pitcher plants. These incredible plant species are carnivorous.

Pitcher plants do not have teeth. Their leaves are shaped like deep pitchers. Insects fly into the leaves looking for nectar. The inside of a pitcher plant's leaf is very slippery. An insect cannot climb out. It gets tired trying to escape. The insect eventually falls to the bottom of the leaf. Liquid at the bottom of the pitcher acts like stomach acid. It breaks down the

The bottom of a pitcher plant contains liquid that breaks down the bodies of the plant's prey.

16
Height, in inches (41 cm), of the pitcher of the biggest species of pitcher plant, *Nepenthes rajah*.

- Pitcher plants trap and break down insects and other animals for energy.
- The leaves of the pitcher plant are shaped like pitchers.
- Liquid at the bottom of the leaf digests a pitcher plant's prey.

insect's body. The plant uses this food for energy.

Insects are not the only pitcher plant prey. Depending on its size, a pitcher plant will eat anything. It could be a fly, a frog, or even a rat. Some pitcher plant species eat animal poop. An enormous pitcher plant grows in the Philippines. It gets nutrients from rodent poop. The rodent sits on the edge of the plant. It eats the plant's nectar. As it eats, it poops into the pitcher. The liquid at the bottom of the plant's pitcher breaks down the poop. The plant gets the nutrients it needs.

GOOD RELATIONSHIPS

The giant pitcher plant and the rodent have a mutually beneficial relationship. The two different species work together to get something they both need. Insects and birds also have this type of relationship with plants. The animals eat the plants' nectar and seeds. They get the food they need. In doing so, they spread the plants' pollen and seeds. This ensures there will be more plants in the future.

Rafflesia Is the Largest and Smelliest Flower

The Rafflesia is the largest flower in the world. It grows in Southeast Asia. This incredible plant has no leaves, stems, or true roots. It is just a flower. And it smells like death.

The Rafflesia flower is a parasite. It relies on other plants for the nutrients it needs for survival. A grapevine is usually a Rafflesia's host. The Rafflesia hides inside the grapevine's roots and stems. It waits until it is ready to reproduce. Then a large, round bud bursts through the grapevine's bark. Five giant reddish-orange petals unfurl around a large center cup.

The bud of a Rafflesia flower

42

Average diameter, in inches (107 cm), of the Rafflesia flower.

- The Rafflesia flower has no roots, stems, or leaves.
- This parasitic plant gets its nutrients from a host plant, usually a grapevine.
- The Rafflesia smells like rotting meat, which attracts flies that spread its pollen.

A giant Rafflesia flower blooms atop a rotting log.

The Rafflesia flower goes by another name, too. It is also known as the corpse flower. Its cup smells like rotting meat. There is a good reason for the flower's stinky smell. Carrion flies are insects that eat dead animals. They land on the Rafflesia's enormous flower. Their bodies pick up the Rafflesia's pollen. The pollen falls off the insects' bodies as they fly. The spread of pollen helps the flower reproduce.

PARASITIC PLANTS

Parasitic plants are common. The Australian Christmas Tree cuts into other plants' roots. It steals these plants' water. Mistletoe grows on trees. It cuts into its host tree's branches and trunk. It steals the tree's nutrients. Eventually, the tree dies.

Rainbow Eucalyptus Tree Reveals Multicolored Bark

The rainbow eucalyptus tree is a striking plant. It certainly lives up to its name. Its tall, thick trunk is streaked with green, orange, red, and purple.

Rainbow eucalyptus trees are tropical plants. They need warm weather and moist soil to survive. The trees are native to Papua New Guinea and Indonesia. They have broad, shiny green leaves. A rainbow eucalyptus tree can double in size each year. It can grow more than 200 feet (61 m) tall.

The tree sheds its bark throughout the year. When a strip falls off, new bark is revealed

A stand of rainbow eucalyptus trees brightens the landscape in Maui, Hawaii.

The streaks of color of rainbow eucalyptus bark look painted on.

33

Height, in feet (10 m), a rainbow eucalyptus tree can grow in just 18 months.

- The rainbow eucalyptus tree has colorful bark.
- The bark changes colors the longer it is exposed to air.
- The tree sheds its bark at different rates, revealing many different colors at once.

underneath. As the tree ages, its bark changes colors. Freshly revealed bark is bright green. After it has been exposed for 20 years, it turns a pale reddish brown. The tree sheds its bark at different rates. This creates the rainbow of colors that gives the tree its name.

Saltstraumen Swirls in the Norwegian Sea

Pull the plug on the bathtub and watch the water whirl down. See how it spirals toward the drain? That is a whirlpool. Natural whirlpools exist in oceans and rivers all over the world.

Moving water changes direction when it encounters something in its path. This could be a rock or a piece of land. It could even be another current from other moving water. If the water is moving fast enough, it will twist around itself or the other current. This twisting forms a whirlpool.

The strongest whirlpool in the world is *Saltstraumen*, or salt current. It is in the Norwegian Sea near Bodø, Norway.

Saltstraumen occurs at the opening of a Norwegian fjord.

23

Speed, in miles per hour (37 km/h), of the Saltstraumen current.

- Whirlpools are created when rushing water runs into something, such as land or another current.
- Norway's Saltstraumen is the strongest whirlpool in the world.
- Water rushes into the narrow Skjerstad fjord at high tide, causing the whirlpool.

The phenomenon has existed for more than 2,000 years. During high tide, 400 million tons (363 million metric t) of seawater rush into the narrow Skjerstad Fjord. The rush of water creates Saltstraumen.

Whirlpools form as the water in the fjord evens out with the water level of the sea. The swirl can be up to 33 feet (10 m) wide. It grows to be 16 feet (4.9 m) deep. It does not last forever, though.

When the current slows and the tide recedes, the Saltstraumen current disappears. It will re-form when the tide rises again.

Saltstraumen whirlpools form where water from the fjord meets the incoming tide.

Volcanic Rock Formed Giant's Causeway

Giant's Causeway is a four-mile (6.4-km) stretch of enormous rocks. The rocks jut out of the Irish Sea. Their size is impressive. But their most striking feature is their shape.

Each rock is an individual pillar. Each pillar is between 15 and 20 inches (38 and 51 cm) in diameter. Some are nearly 85 feet (26 m) tall. Most of the pillars have six sides. Others have as few as five or as many as eight sides.

The unique shape of these rocky cliffs makes them look as if they were carved by a giant. But they are actually the work of a volcano. Sixty million years ago, the area was covered in melted rock called lava.

Giant's Causeway stones get their shape from volcanic activity.

The lava cooled into rock. The lava at the top and bottom of the valley cooled at different rates. This created the long, vertical cracks in the rock. It separated the rock into pillars.

Wind and rain carved a valley into the rock. The valley was filled with more lava. Over time, a glacier and rising seas wore away any roughness. Today, the rocks of Giant's Causeway have a smooth surface. It is easy to imagine a giant creating them.

Many of the stones appear to be made by hand, but nature gave them their shape.

THE LEGEND OF FINN MCCOOL

Giant's Causeway was first recorded in the 1600s. People did not know if it was made by humans or nature. Some suspected it was the work of giants. Local legend said an Irish giant, Finn McCool, created the causeway. He built it as a bridge between Ireland and Scotland.

40,000
Number of pillars that make up Giant's Causeway.

- Giant's Causeway is a large group of rock pillars along the coast of the Irish Sea.
- Lava from a volcano created the rocks 60 million years ago.
- Lava hardened into rock that was later made smooth by a glacier and rising seawater.

Fact Sheet

- The water cycle begins with rain. As rain falls, it goes into rivers, lakes, oceans, and the ground. Heat from the sun makes some of that water evaporate, or turn into a gas. That is water vapor. Water vapor rises into the air. As it cools, it turns back into tiny drops of liquid and forms clouds. When a cloud is heavy with water droplets, gravity pulls it down in the form of rain.

- Plants make their own food through photosynthesis. Light, carbon dioxide, and water are needed for this process. Plants absorb carbon dioxide through tiny pores on their leaves. The plant draws water from the soil through its roots. It converts light from the sun into energy. The water uses this energy to split the carbon dioxide molecules. The result is a simple sugar that feeds the plant. Photosynthesis helps humans and other animals, too. The process creates oxygen, something all creatures need to survive.

- Plants also pull nutrients, such as nitrogen, from the soil. But not all soil has enough nutrients for all plants. Some plants have changed over time to fix this problem. Carnivorous plants catch small animals, such as insects. They kill the animals and then remove nutrients from them such as iron and protein. Other plants are parasites. Parasitic plants do little or no photosynthesis. They rely on other plants to deliver water and nutrients.

- The crust of planet Earth is made up of many different kinds of rocks. When wind, water, and living things interact with rocks, it causes weathering. This shapes the rocks into new forms. Sometimes, rocks are re-melted and new rocks are made. Other times, rocks are slowly dissolved away by either hot or cold water. Hot springs and caves are both examples of places where water dissolves rock. Dissolved rock can then help to re-form as different minerals, or even huge crystals.

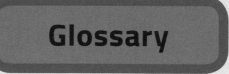

Glossary

atmosphere
All the gases surrounding Earth.

bioluminescence
A chemical process that makes some living things glow.

carnivorous
Trapping and breaking down animal matter for energy.

evaporates
Changes from a liquid to a gas.

fjord
A narrow sea channel between two cliffs.

molecules
The smallest parts of a particular substance, such as oxygen.

nutrients
Substances in food that support life.

parasite
Something that relies on another living thing to survive.

particles
Very small pieces of matter.

pigments
Colored matter created by some plants and animals.

playa
Flat, dry desert land that sometimes serves as the floor of a quickly forming, shallow lake.

predator
An animal that kills and eats another animal.

prey
An animal that is killed and eaten by another animal.

For More Information

Books

Beer, Amy-Jane. *Cool Nature: 50 Fantastic Facts for Kids of All Ages*. London: Pavilion, 2016.

Honovich, Nancy. *Rocks & Minerals*. Washington, DC: National Geographic, 2016.

Jones, Keisha. *Plants That Eat*. New York: PowerKids, 2017.

Visit 12StoryLibrary.com

Scan the code or use your school's login at **12StoryLibrary.com** for recent updates about this topic and a full digital version of this book. Enjoy free access to:

- Digital ebook
- Breaking news updates
- Live content feeds
- Videos, interactive maps, and graphics
- Additional web resources

Note to educators: Visit 12StoryLibrary.com/register to sign up for free premium website access. Enjoy live content plus a full digital version of every 12-Story Library book you own for every student at your school.

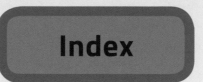

Index

About the Author

Kristin Marciniak researches and writes from her home in Overland Park, Kansas, where she lives with her husband, son, and golden retriever.

READ MORE FROM 12-STORY LIBRARY

Every 12-Story Library book is available in many formats. For more information, visit 12StoryLibrary.com.